WHAT DO YOU DO?

HOW TO GROW YOUR BUSINESS BY ANSWERING THE RIGHT WAY

WESLEY YOUNG

FOREWORD BY BROOKE ZRNO GRISHAM

American

oneworld

BAGGAGE CHARGE RECEIPT

PASSENGER NAME
ROSSI/NINA MARIE RONQUILLO   1   25.00 USD

UPTO50LB 23KG AND62LI

                                               25.00 USD

SFO DFW - AA
Total with Applicable TFC
          MC xxxxxxxxxxxx0261
Credit Card

FLIGHT   DATE
1191   MAY 02, 2017   0280769532

PNR: HPUNFG
Agent: SFO-SSM   001   4

Fare   25.00 USD
TFC
TFC
TFC   25.00 USD
Total

TFC=TAXES,FEES & CHARGES

NOT VALID FOR TRAVEL

- DEDICATION -

This book is dedicated to my father, Terry Young. I have learned, and continue to learn, so many wonderful things from him. As I was finishing this book, I began to think about all the hours reading and listening to audios that I have consumed over the years and how this time shaped how I think and move in business. My father taught me to always intentionally develop my thinking to a higher level. He did this not by speeches, but by example. My father spent a lot of time driving from one store to the next in his business. There was not a time when I didn't see him with an audio book queued up with the intention of making him a better father, husband, friend or leader. He is indeed great in all of these roles. Thanks Dad!

- TABLE OF CONTENTS -

WHAT PEOPLE ARE SAYING ABOUT
WHAT DO YOU DO?

"The brilliance of Wes Young is his ability to take some of the most complicated subjects and break them down to reasonable and simplistic solutions that can easily be replicated. His language, in line with his incredible passion and belief, are powerful enough to enroll and engage the reader into a new way of looking at their most challenging issues. The first 7 seconds can make or break a new relationship. We can arm anyone, making those 7 seconds powerful and memorable. The content of this book will bring countless riches to the reader if implemented."

MICHAEL F. SCOVEL CLU®, ChFC®, MSM

MANAGING PARTNER, NEW YORK LIFE DALLAS GENERAL OFFICE

"Wes has taken a complicated and confusing process (engaging people in the act of financial planning) and broken it down to the most critical essentials. In a world of labels and similarity, he shows us how to be unique and valuable. His well thought language and processes help advisors see and think more powerfully, which allows us to help our clients do the same."

RYAN M. DAUS, CFP®, CHFC®, CLU

PRESIDENT, DAUS FINANCIAL GROUP, LL

"Wes Young has created a great playbook that will help Financial Advisors of all experience levels answer one of the most important and fundamental questions we face; "What do you do?" Wes's humor, the use of analogies and ability to articulate make this a must read for any advisor that wants to get to the next level."

JOSEPH D. KRUSE, CLU®, ChFC®, CFP®, AE

PRESIDENT, KRUSE FINANCIAL GROUP

"Wes has hit the nail on the head with "Problem to Avoid or Opportunity to Seize". The book is full of Little Pearls of wisdom that any practitioner can quickly deploy into their respective practice and see immediate results. Wes is wise beyond his years and the insight we are able to pick up in the book is a testament to that; wonderful addition to anyone's Business reading library."

GIB SURLES, CLU®, ChFC®, CFP®, AEP, MSF

FOUNDER, THE FORREST GROUP, LL

"This book is a gem. Not only because it addresses issues many advisers face-but because it aids in formulating a solution that is customized to you and the people you serve. After reading this book , you will have clarity and direction on how to answer the question that is the most challenging for many producers. Learning this process will allow you not only to create an excellent "first Impression,' but a foundation for strong relationships and a better business model. I would recommend this book to any financial entrepreneur who is seeking to take their practice to the next level."

TAYLOR M. SLEDGE, JR.

FOUNDER, SLEDGE & COMPANY

This book is a must read for all business owners! Most of us get the question, "So what do you do?" all the time, and Wes's advice on how to turn your answer into a new business opportunity is spot on."

KELLY EDWARDS

CEO, LAWTON MARKETING GROUP

WHAT DO YOU DO?

WHAT DO YOU DO?

- FOREWORD -

A frequent question I have been asked over the years goes something like, "What does Wes Young do and say, and how can I do the same?" When you pull back the curtain on Wes as a business owner, you find one common driver: intentionality of thought. Nothing Wes has accomplished resulted from chance or luck. Rather, his success is a direct result of planning, building, testing, and the ability to implement... with intention.

In his book, you will find the architectural plans and the keys to build your own house of success. Wes has clearly emerged as a thought leader in the financial industry, on not just the tangible ways in which advisors continue to grow; but also the intangible importance of intentional thought.

Beyond Wes as a business owner, is Wes as a teacher and coach. It is in these pages where he inspires the reader to take a step back from the day-to-day obligations, and consider a new way of thinking and approach. It is here where Wes shares his intentional journey. And it is here, where you will find your own business transformation-taking place.

BROOKE ZRNO GRISHAM, ChFC®, CLU®, AEP

CEO, THE NAUTILUS GROUP®

WHAT DO YOU DO?

- PART 1 -

PROBLEM TO SOLVE OR OPPORTUNITY TO SEIZE?
Discovering one of our greatest untapped opportunities

- PROBLEM TO SOLVE OR OPPORTUNITY TO SEIZE? -

Have you ever heard the story of the two shoe salesmen? It goes like this; two shoe salesmen fly to an island in hopes of expanding their businesses. After a full day of surveying the market, each salesman sent word home. The first salesman said, "Bad news! No one on the island wears shoes. I'll be back home tomorrow."

The second salesman said, "Great news! No one on the island wears shoes! I'll be staying another month." Isn't it interesting how each man took a reality, (no one on the island wears shoes), and one of them saw this as a problem to avoid, while the other saw it as an opportunity to seize?

I believe there is a great, untapped opportunity we have available to us in the financial planning business. Unfortunately, many great advisers will miss out on it, simply because they view it as a problem to avoid rather than an opportunity to seize. This opportunity arises in the form of the question, "What do you do?"

Do you know what I am talking about? You're on an airplane, at a party or on an elevator and they spring it on you, "So, what do you do?" How many times have you walked away from answering that question and thought, "Man, I really missed that opportunity"? Why is it so difficult for us to answer that question in a way that allows us to feel good? I think one legitimate reason is, unlike all or our other meetings we have during the week, we never know when the "What Do You Do?" meeting is coming. Thus, we are unprepared. All of our other meetings go on the calendar, and we spend focused time preparing what we want to communicate. As the time of our meeting draws near, the "What Do You Do?" meeting seems to spring itself on you like a thief in the night. Let's be honest, even if you knew the question was coming, it probably wouldn't help you much. What if I could tell you that at 1:00 tomorrow you are going to get on an elevator full of billionaires that haven't done any planning, and one of them is going to ask you what you do? Even with hours to prepare, most advisers wouldn't have an answer they were excited about nor would it have led to the kind of response they hoped for. If you have been in this business long enough you have probably had lots of answers to this question.

For most of them you "chickened out" of, never used, or couldn't remember. When you finally used one that you thought fully captured what you did, you discovered it was so long that by the time you were done saying it either the party was over, or the elevator had gone up and down five times. It's likely that you eventually settled on something you didn't really like and didn't produce the results you were looking for, you just didn't know any other way. In essence you became like shoe salesman number one.

You began to see the "What Do You Do?" meeting as a problem to avoid rather than an opportunity to seize.

It is my hope that this book gives you what you need to flip that perspective, to begin to see the "What Do You Do?" meeting as an opportunity to seize rather than a problem to avoid. In fact, I believe this is one of the greatest untapped opportunities for progress that exists in our industry. Every year we take on over half of our new clients as a result of being great at answering this question. Not only does our approach to answering this question lead us to more clients, but it also enhances the quality of the relationships we have with clients. Answering this question powerfully creates a very different atmosphere for the clients. The ripple effect of doing this extends to the furthest reaches of your business.

- BOOK REPORTS AND LABELS -

Before I dive into our approach to the "What Do You Do" meeting I want to take a minute to explore the most common approaches. Normally when we are asked the question "What do you do?" we give a book report or a label.

When I was about a year into the business and I sat in a Starbucks for four hours with my friend, Chris, we tried to capture a dynamic answer to the *"What Do You Do?"* question. We wanted to give an answer that didn't put us in the predetermined box. While we may have carried a similar title to the other people that are in our industry, we didn't want them to think we offered the same experience as them. We wrote and wrote and wrote and our answer to this question was so long that we would have needed an elevator that was nine times as tall as the Empire State Building to get it all out. It was very long and complicated. When we attempted to use our speech we would forget our words and stumble over them. It did succeed in regard to separating us from the others in our industry, just not in a good way. After many failed attempts, we became unhappy with the results of the book "report approach" and resigned ourselves to the opposite extreme. We gave ourselves labels like, financial adviser, insurance agent, or money manager.

Here is the problem. Labels go on boxes, and the last thing you want is to be put in a pre-constructed box before someone has experienced your brand of value. The problem with giving a label like "insurance agent", "money manager", or "financial adviser", is it says nothing about what you do. In fact, it presupposes the person has a definition for these labels. It also reinforces the idea they are all the same. By giving a label as an answer to the question, you give prospects permission to believe what you do is the same thing someone else they know with the same label does. In essence, it is likely they have a box in their mind with the label financial advisor on it. When you answer the question, "What do you do?" with a label, then you are really saying is, "Do you know what a financial adviser does? I do that too, so please put me in the box you put all other financial advisers."

This way of answering lacks power, because it gives the person permission to assume you are like everyone else they know who uses that title. At best, the prospect may like the person they already know who carries the title. While they may think of you favorably, they also think of you as common. You are just like whom they already know. At worst, they don't like the experience they have had with others; they view you as common and someone they don't want to be around.

In the end, both of these approaches fail to get the kind of results you are hoping for. You begin to look at the "*What Do You Do?*" question just like shoe salesman number one, as a problem to avoid. But here is the good news; it doesn't have to be this way. There is an approach that doesn't involve labels or book reports. Like I said earlier, this approach not only increases the quantity of clients we take on but the quality of the client relationships we have. It has a ripple effect throughout our entire practice. So what is this new approach to the "*What Do You Do*" meeting? It is the "Why Before What Approach".

- WHY BEFORE WHAT -

As children, there is a question we are genetically prewired to ask from birth, "Why?" As a parent, it is easy to get frustrated when I tell Gage or Abby to do something like brush their teeth or clean up the room. Rather than obedience I get the question, "Why?" In my frustration, I give them an answer that I'll bet is pretty similar to the one you give your children, "Because I said so!"

But that's not the real reason, is it? For instance, the real reason I want them to brush their teeth is because I don't want them to experience the pain of getting a cavity filled.

One day, I thought rather than lead with "What" and I would start with "Why." We had just finished dinner one night and rather than make the statement I always made, "Go brush your teeth", I started with a question: "Hey kids! You know how you hate going to the doctor when he has to put needles in your arms?"

To which Gage and Abby looked at me with a kind of fearful curiosity and said, "Yes?"

Then I responded, "Did you know brushing your teeth every day helps keep the dentist from having to stick needles in your gums?" What happened next was amazing: they both, unprompted, got up from the table and brushed their teeth. It was at this point that I knew I was on to something. The difference between resistance and passionate acceptance, in this case, was that I gave them the "Why" before I gave them the "What." In fact, they pursued the "What" on their own when given a compelling enough "Why."

The truth buried in this exercise is this:
The people you are trying to lead need to feel the weight of the problem you are trying to solve, before you give solutions and directives.

I began to look at ways to integrate this into my conversations with clients and eventually into my "What Do You Do?" meeting. People may ask, "What do you do?" Rather than help them feel the weight of the problem that we solve with a question, we give them a label or a book report on the activities of our job. We essentially give them "What" without a compelling "Why." The key element that's missing is the "Why" behind the "What." To make the biggest impact in our ability to connect with people in a helpful way, we must know the "Why" behind our "What" and be able to convey that in the form of a question.

A good answer to our "What Do You Do?" is not about statements or labels but rather about our "Why" in doing "What" we do.

In fact, being able to answer this question from the "Why" perspective will not only enable you to engage more opportunities that fit you best, but it will enable you to shape your entire process around it. I like what Rick Warren, author of the great book *The Purpose Driven Life* said; "Knowing your purpose (your Why) simplifies your life. It defines what you do and what you don't do. Your purpose (or your Why) becomes the standard you use to evaluate which activities are essential and which aren't. You simply ask, 'Does this activity help me fulfill one of God's purposes for my life?'" He goes on to say, "People who don't know their purpose try to do too much-and that causes stress, fatigue, and conflict."

Without a clear "Why," we get into a rhythm of life that pursues as many "Whats" as we possibly can. We spend our time finding work and doing it rather than knowing our "Why" and pursuing it.

Let me give you an example of how we answer this question. Then, we will break down the pattern for delivery and the questions you have. This will allow you to shape effective content for delivery.

NOTES

- WHAT DO YOU DO? FRAMING IT UP -

My response when someone asks what I do is, "Well you know how we have a tendency to run out of time before we run out of all the ideas and opportunities we want to pursue?"

To which almost 100% of the time they respond, "Yes, I know exactly what you mean."

Then I reply, "I help people with that. I own a financial planning company. We help people who own businesses identify and pursue their best financial opportunities."

Usually, if I have a qualified candidate for business, they will respond with "Interesting, how do you do that?" At this point, the environment I am in will dictate the appropriate next step.

If I am at a party, I will arrange for another meeting by saying the following, "Well, we start by asking a lot of questions to understand where you are from a financial standpoint and the types of things that are important to you. Once we know that, we can have a good conversation about the areas of planning we specialize in that may be most valuable to what you're trying to accomplish. Why don't we connect next week and I can show you."

If I am on an airplane, I may tweak it to set up our next meeting right there by saying something like this, "Well, we start by asking a lot of questions to understand where you are from a financial standpoint and the types of things that are important to you. Once we know your objectives, we can have a good conversation about the areas of planning we specialize in that may be most valuable to what you're trying to accomplish. If you'd like, I can show you right now since we have some time."

Almost every time I'm asked how I do that, I move forward with another meeting. Here is the pattern for delivering a great answer to the question, "What Do You Do?"

Step 1: *State the core problem you solve in the form of a question.*

Step 2: *Associate yourself with the solution simply and specifically.*

Step 3: *Give an easy transition to action.*

STEP 1: State the core problem you solve in the form of a question.

"Well, you know how we all tend to run out of time before we run out of all the ideas and opportunities we want to pursue?"

Notice how rather than start with a statement or a label we engage the client with a question. The reason for this is two fold:

First, starting with a question changes the dynamic of the What Do You Do meeting from a presentation to conversation. For years, when I would try to answer this question it felt like I was on stage and the prospect said, "dance!" I would dance my best dance and could only hope they would ask me to dance again. In essence, it felt like a one-way presentation. Starting with a question completely changes the dynamic enabling you go from presentation to conversation. A good question invites the prospect to dance with you instead of dancing alone.

Second, the prospect needs to feel the weight of the problem you are trying to solve before you give solutions. The reason some of the most incredible phrasing of statements about what we do don't get any traction is because we start with a lot of what and how instead of starting with why any of those things matter. It's not that you are creating a problem for them. You are making them aware of a problem they already know exists. Most ongoing problems we learn to live with and push out of our mind as a reality we must endure. The moment someone brings that problem to the surface, the weight of that problem becomes front and center seeking a solution. In a later section, I will give you the thought process behind the problem we solve, our "Why." For now, lets move on to the next step in a great *"What Do You Do?"* meeting.

STEP 2: Associate yourself with the solution simply and specifically.

I help people with that. I own a financial planning company; we work with people who own businesses to help them identify and pursue their best financial opportunities.

Now you are ready to help the prospect associate you with the solution to their problem. Start with a very simple statement like, "I help people with that." Then, get very specific (as to the realm you work in) because you don't want them to walk away with the wrong idea. Say something like, "I own a financial planning company; we help business owners identify and pursue their best financial opportunities."

This step allows you to create a new box in their mind for what you do. Regardless of what your label is, they associate you with the solution to a problem. What's great is you don't match any of the existing boxes they have in their mind. You started helping them feel the weight of the problem and then associated yourself as the solution to the problem. Your relational influence and credibility skyrockets in value as a result. Many clients we engage already have a financial adviser, money manager, or insurance agent. Associating us as solution to their problem created a new category of adviser; and they chose to hire us.

STEP 3: Give an easy transition to action.

We start by asking a lot of questions to understand where you are from a financial standpoint, and the types of things that are important to you. Once we know these things, we can have a good conversation about the areas of planning we specialize in that may be most valuable to what you're trying to accomplish. Why don't we connect next week and I can show you.

I will only say this statement if the person I am speaking with invites me to do so. To use a fishing analogy, the first part of what I have been doing is putting out "chum." For the non-fisherman readers, "chum" is cut or ground bait dumped into the water to attract fish to the area where one is fishing. If the prospect doesn't have a strong enough attraction to what I have been putting out, I am not interested in forcing them to hang around for more, I will go fishing elsewhere.

On the other hand, if they like what I have been putting out, I am more than happy to keep the conversation going. The way I know that they want to continue is they will ask, "How do you do that?"

Before moving on from here, I want to point out that this is the style that fits my personality. There are many different personality styles in the world and it may fit your personality just fine to move ahead with a transition to action even if they don't ask, "How do you do that?" I have plenty of friends from the northeast that are, to use another fishing analogy, more like noodlers than chum fisherman. Noodlers are people who do not wait for the fish to be attracted to what they are putting out. They jump into the water and stick their arms in mud holes along the bank of a river or lake and jam their arm into the fish's mouth in hopes of yanking it to the surface. I know it sounds like I am making this up but just watch the Discovery Channel long enough and you will get to see it. Some of my friends take this approach with telling people how they do what they do and are still successful. However, it does create a different environment for the meetings you have going forward that I am just unwilling to manage.

NOTES

WHAT DO YOU DO?

- PART 2 -

MAKE IT FIT - THE FOUR ESSENTIAL ELEMENTS

Customizing your personal approach

- MAKING IT FIT -

Years ago, I was checking out with a pair of dress pants at a men's clothing store when the clerk said, "Sir, it's your lucky day. These pants are actually on sale for fifteen dollars each and I have two more pairs in the back if you would like them."

To which I responded, "Sure! I'll take them!" A few moments later the clerk emerged with the pants and began to ring them up when I noticed a problem, they were size forty-two and I wear a size thirty-two. So, naturally, I brought this to his attention. I said, "Hey these aren't going to work for me, they are size forty-two."

Then the clerk leaned over the counter and as if he were letting me in on an insider's secret, he said in a kind of whisper, "Yea, but they're only fifteen bucks, its still a great deal."

The funny thing is, for a minute I thought, "Yea, he's right, that is a good deal, I should take them!" Thankfully I came to my senses and did not buy the pants. No matter how good a deal they were, it didn't make them fit.

I bring up this story to highlight the fact that, though we have just unpacked a great pattern for delivering the "*What Do You Do?*" discussion, it will not produce the kind of results you want unless you tailor it to fit your practice. For some people that may mean saying exactly what I say, but for others saying what I say would be like wearing size forty-two pants when you are a size thirty-two, it just won't fit you. In this section of the book we are going to wrestle out four very important elements to customizing the content you deliver in the
"*What Do You Do?*" meeting. As always, I'll give you our approach to each of these along the way.

- THE FOUR ESSENTIALS ELEMENTS -

Here are the four elements essential to the "What Do You Do?" meeting: "What" and "Why," "Who" and "How." You can have the greatest delivery method in the world, but answering these questions helps you understand what you're trying to deliver. In essence, it is the cargo you carry. One of the greatest byproducts of doing the work to answer this question is that your practice becomes very purpose driven. You will know What you do, Why you do it, Who you do it for and How you do it.

People who don't regularly take the time to answer these questions operate in a kind of "fog." Rather than operate out of clear, purpose driven activity, their purpose becomes to look for work and do it. Your best opportunities for success come from knowing your purpose and pursuing it, no just looking for work and doing it. Clearly defining your purpose becomes the framework by which you evaluate opportunities. This clear definition will help you to look for those opportunities that fit you best and say "no" or delegate the rest. The "Why" before "What" approach has a great ripple effect throughout your practice of making it very purpose driven and genuine. Lets take a look at each one.

- WHAT & WHY - A BUMPER STICKER WIN -

"What" is a question that refers to "What is my win with my clients?" From a big picture standpoint, "What" is it that I want them to walk away and do as a result of our interaction together? When it comes to my "What", I am not looking for a mission statement that explains everything, but more of a tagline that summarizes my win when it comes to our clients. Of course there will be a long explanation to create your "What," but the goal is to get it down to as few words as possible. It should be portable and memorable, almost like a statement you would see on a bumper sticker.

Our bumper sticker win is: ***Helping People Create More Than They Consume.***

We will spend the next three questions helping you understand how we came to tha win.

"Why" refers to the purpose or the point of my win. This is the motivation behind the win. In other words, what core problem does your win solve, or what opportunity does your win seize? It is also helpful to summarize your "Why" in a brief statement. Having one central statement that summarizes the "Why" explanation is essential to it sticking in the hearts and minds of people. Many times in our attempt to be thorough and complete we are not memorable. Honestly, what is the point of being thorough and complete if no one remembers what you said? This is not an easy exercise but it is critical to your ability to seize the opportunities that fit you best.

For us, the bumper sticker statements of "What" and "Why" came after a bunch of thinking and writing; and we are constantly trying to tweak and refine it. Don't get overwhelmed by trying to make it perfect, just make it clear and continue to refine and work on it.

Our "Why" statement: ***We will all run out of time and money before we run out of ideas and opportunities.***

The explanation behind our "Why" statement: We all have far more ideas we want o pursue than we have money and time to pursue those ideas. In essence we will un out of time before we run out of opportunities. It is in this statement that the problem or opportunity emerges.

As evidenced by their continuous attempt to out run and out earn all their ideas, people don't live as if this is true. This mode of operation never leads to the life they re looking for, but rather it leads to exhaustion. Financially, it leads to a life where hey are consuming everything they create in an effort to get on the other side of heir ideas.

he reason most people have little financial margin is not because they don't make nough money; it is because they have not learned to create more than they onsume with what they have. The reason **"Helping people create more than they onsume"** is our win is because most people allow their ideas to consume all they reate both financially and physically. They view the gap between where they are nd where they want to be as a problem to solve. They continue to throw all their ime and money at it in an attempt to solve the problem.

he issue with this view is your gap never goes away, it just moves. The gap is never ully and finally satisfied. While it cannot be satisfied, we can learn to embrace it as n adventure to be pursued, rather than a problem to be solved. One of the ways we o this is by **helping people create more than they consume** right where they are on heir way to where they are going.

ater, you'll learn about our Four-Phase Process that we take our clients through to ccomplish this. We will continue to expand on this in the next section.

Ve believe that creating more than you consume is the most powerful definition of rich" that a person can possess. In fact, I wrote a book on the matter called "From usy to Rich" that you can purchase on Amazon. We will continue to expand on this hinking in the next section.

NOTES

_____

_____

_____

_____

_____

_____

_____

_____

_____

_____

_____

_____

_____

_____

_____

_____

_____

_____

_____

- WHO - WHERE ARE THEY RELATIVE TO RICH? -

"Who" refers to the target market for the "What" you are delivering. In light of your win, at your current level of capacity and competence, "Who" are you best equipped to serve? Another great question to evaluate here is, "Do I have influence with the people that I am identifying as my "Who"?

When I first got into the financial business, I wanted to work with successful business owners. The challenge was I did not have the competence to do so. I also did not have much influence with that market at that time so my opportunity to deliver my win to that group was not very good. While I worked on building my competence and my influence with my target audience, I worked with the audience that I did have competence and influence with. I spent a lot of time at night teaching people who were consuming everything they were creating how to get health financially. I would put term life insurance in place to protect them if they died on their way to getting financially healthy. Eventually, I began to have opportunities to help business owners (who were no longer just surviving), solve their problems, and my influence continued to increase with that audience.

To best identify your "Who", it helps to define segments of the potential market you could serve and what makes them different. We segment our clients according to the following question, "Where are they relative to rich?"

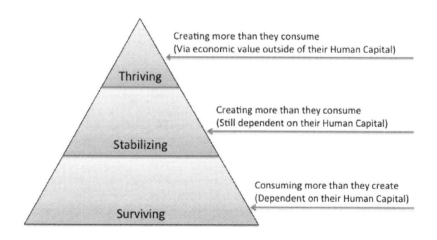

- SURVIVING -

In regard to being rich, someone who is surviving is consuming as much or more than they create; they are living paycheck to paycheck. While this is not always the case, most of the time their thinking will reveal their balance sheet long before they give you their numbers. If you ask them "What do you think is keeping you from being rich?"

They will most likely answer, "I just need more money."

This is simply not true. **More money makes you more of what you already are.** If you don't know how to create more than you consume with what you have, more will just get you further out of balance.

If you do an Internet search for *Curse of the Lottery*, you will read countless stories of lottery winners that are a tragic example of this truth. They were barely surviving off of their income and then they won the lottery, only to find they are bankrupt just a few years later. The key to this is, understanding that the amount of money or assets a person has does not determine whether they are in surviving, stabilizing or thriving mode. The key is to ask the question, "Are they creating more than they consume?"

One of the greatest barriers to progress and breakthrough is the thought that more money is the cause of prosperity. More money is a byproduct of prosperity, never the cause of it.

As long as someone thinks that more money is the source of financial prosperity, they will not seek out the priorities that actually produce it. Absent of the priorities that lead to prosperity, they will spend their days in pursuit of more of something they are totally unfit to handle. The rhythm of life they fall into is one of perpetual pursuit without priorities.

If someone has an idea and does not have the financial capacity to make that idea a reality, he tends to look for the easiest way to get the financial means to make it happen. In our current culture the easiest answer has been to "spend all I have and borrow the rest." This would be fine if this were the last idea this man ever had in his head to pursue, and nothing changed in a negative direction financially. However, this man will soon have another idea to pursue, and then another that screams even louder in his mind. In fact, the endless stream of ideas that will continue to come to this man's mind will far exceed his financial and physical capacity to pursue them all. To further complicate matters, his financial situation will change, and it doesn't have to change much to corrupt a foundation for progress that is made up of "spending all I have and borrowing the rest." People in survival mode are often slaves to this way of thinking, rather than take responsibility for their circumstances; they blame their lack of money.

- STABILIZING & THRIVING -

People in either the stabilizing and thriving seasons of life have something in common; they are both creating more than they consume financially. The difference is that, those who are stabilizing are dependent on their human capital to continue to create more than they consume. In other words, they need to trade time for money to continue to create more than they consume.

Those who are thriving have built enough economic value outside of themselves (in liquid and/or business assets) and, structured their expenses in such a way that they will continue to continue to create more than they consume whether they are trading their time for money or not. In other words, their ability to create more than they consume is no longer dependent on their human capital. This does not mean they are finished making financial decisions; none of the distinctions we have discussed are a position of permanence. We are all a few decisions away from moving from one position to another, both positively or negatively.

There are variations of people in each category. Those who are saving even one dollar more then they consume have barely crossed the line into stabilizing in regard to rich; while someone who has been saving for a long time, (and has built up liquidity capable of producing more income than they consume), has crossed over the line into thriving. You could also have a business owner who is able to create more than they consume by showing up and keeping their business running well every day. However, if they were to stop showing up, the business would no longer continue to run well; this person is stabilizing. However, if the business owner has built enough value in the business to where it continues to create more than he consumes, even in his extended absence, then he is thriving in regard to rich.

In our first interactions with potential business relationships, I want to have a process that helps me understand where they are in regard to rich. The reason is simple but so often overlooked. Though all financial information I possess may be true, not all financial information I possess is applicable for the season of life a person is in. Let me give you an example by way of a funny story about my daughter Abby.

When Abby was four, she played indoor soccer at the YMCA. When we signed her up, the league fell under the heading of "organized children's athletics." We found this very funny because if you have ever seen four year olds play soccer, you will find nothing organized about it. It is, basically, like watching a swarm of bees chasing after a ball. No one plays defense, and you spend the majority of the game watching the one skilled child on each team score goals. The coach of our team had coaching experience at some of the highest levels of soccer. The reason he was now coaching four year olds was that his four-year-old son was on the team.

I will never forget what happened one practice as the coach decided he was going to teach my daughter defense. He pulled Abby aside and began to explain how important it was that she played defense, and not just chase the ball like all the other kids. He told her what it would mean to the team, how they would win games, and began to explain the nuances of defense. To my surprise, he seemed to have her attention. Her eyes were locked on his and she even seemed to nod in agreement as he spoke. Then, after he finished his articulate, educational and motivational speech he asked, "Now do you get it?"

To which Abby looked back at him and said, "I am going to wear my Hello Kitty dress to school tomorrow."

In the middle of explosive laughter the coach relented, "Just kick the ball that way."

It's a funny story, but the lesson in it rings true: *Just because something is true, doesn't make it relevant to a season of a person's life.* That is why it is so important to understand where someone is in regard to rich. You may have many great financial strategies, but they may not be relevant for a person's season of life in regard to rich. For instance, you may know all the advanced estate tax law, but someone in survival mode needs to be taught budgeting and have some term insurance put in place. Teaching them about investing or estate taxes is like teaching a four-year old defense; they just need to be taught to kick the ball toward the other net.

In light of your current passions and capacity, where are you best equipped to serve clients, surviving, stabilizing or thriving? Where do most of your clients fit today?

This is your current sweet spot. Of course, this doesn't mean you will be stuck here forever, but it does inform you as to how to best invest your energy today, as well as ask the right question if you want to be in a different sweet spot tomorrow.

It is the dance between "being" and "becoming." Understand "What" you are then ask, "Am I becoming the kind of client I am looking for?" Be great at "What" you are today but become better for tomorrow.

NOTES

- HOW - ORGANIZATION & STRUCTURE -

After you identify your "What, Why and Who," you can begin to focus on "How." Your "How" is made up of the many structures that are organized together to produce progress. To ground this, let's use an analogy of a bicycle. First, all bicycles are organized the same way; two wheels, a seat, handlebars and pedals. While they are all organized the same, they can be structured differently. For example, one bicycle may have tires that are structured with hard, smooth, small tires that are great for going on smooth surfaces. Another bicycle may have fat, rugged, soft tires that are great for going over rough terrain. They are organized the same, but, structured differently. Neither structure is right or wrong; they are simply more powerful relative to the environment in which they are attempting to excel.

When assessing your "How," a big part of it is evaluating the structure of each component in your organization, and evaluating the organization itself. A bicycle is organized with two wheels, and a tricycle is organized with three. Once again, neither one is right nor wrong; one is simply more powerful depending on the capacity of the rider. For instance, when you were two years old, a bicycle would have been useless and a tricycle very powerful. Later, as you and your capacity grew, the bicycle became a much more powerful way to get where you wanted to go. When you evaluate your "How," think in terms of organization and structure; be mindful to ask the question, "In light of my past experience, current reality, and future hopes and dreams, what is the best way to be organized and structured?"

While there is an abundance of core areas that you must take into account to give this question justice, the graphic below, which was graciously provided by my friend Brooke Zrno-Grisham (an expert on organization and structure), will give you some great distinctions to get started.

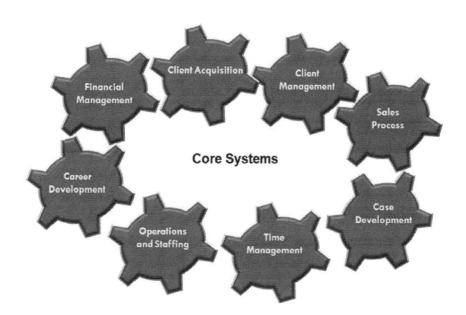

One of the best ways to initially identify your "How," is to think through the process you use to move your ideal client from prospective client to your "Win;" break down each phase of the process then, go back and build the detailed distinctions around it.

NOTES

- PARTING THOUGHT -

MORE TO COME

For now, I will conclude this writing. This will be the first of many more that are likely to come. In future editions or books, I will discuss many of the ideas that our team utilizes in the "Y Approach," an outline is included in the Appendix. My wonderful team at Wes Young & Associates, Stephanie, Cara and Cheryl, has asked me why I don't include this now. The reason is very simple, it takes me time to put ideas in a usable book form and I didn't want to wait any longer to ship out ideas that I have ready to go. So, consider this book the beginning of a journey that will take you to the starting point of the next one. Until then, you can always go in-depth on the other thinking I have referenced by being a part of Planning Shepherd University, with all of our other participants, by calling 866-485-1112 or emailing sales@planningshepherd.com. Until then, I hope you use this little volume to make a very positive impact on all those that need what you do!

Some of the ideas in this book are direct applications of principles and ideas that have grown out of books our team has read and discussed during our weekly team building meetings. Here are some of the books we have read:

From Busy to Rich By Wesley Young
The Holy Bible
7 Practices of Effective Ministry by Andy Stanley, Reggie Joiner & Lane Jones
Purple Cow by Seth Godin
Getting Naked by Patrick Lencioni
Good to Great: Why Some Companies Make the Leap...And Others Don't by Jim Collins
Making Vision Stick by Andy Stanley
Communicating For A Change by Andy Stanley & Lane Jones

- APPENDIX A -

THE "Y APPROACH"
REFERENCE MATERIAL

The following graphs and charts are high-level representations of the Y approach that readers may consider when assessing their own business models and personal philosophies. They are kept intentionally basic to encourage the process of self-discovery. These tools should be considered learning aids in translating the why of this discussion into the how of implementation. You are encouraged to think of these charts as an artist looks at a white canvas before paint is applied. Make them more relevant to your story by writing your own notes in relation to your client interactions and your own business and personal development. There really are no "right" answers in the process of self-discovery, but there are answers that are "right for you." These and future diagrams will be more fully explored in subsequent writings, but I wanted to share some now to add form to theory and to get the conversation started.

NOTES

LOCATION

PREGAME
- Quality Influence
- Prepare Story

WELCOME
- Agenda & Timeline

COMMON GROUND
- What Do You Do Discussion
- Permission To Ask Questions

HEALTHY TENSION
- Discover Their Story Relative To The 3 Reference Points
- Awareness Gap

Conversation Not Interrogation

NEXT STEPS
- Summarize Their Story Relative To The 3 Reference Points
- Next Meeting Request

NOTES

EXPECTATION

PREGAME
- Create Client Project Tracker
- Prepare The Story
- Initial Discovery
- Assemble Relevant Catalyst For Thought

WELCOME
- Agenda & Timeline

COMMON GROUND
- Balance Sheet
- Their Story

HEALTHY TENSION
- (In Light Of) Their Story Relative To The 3 Reference Points
- How Can The Type of Planning We Do Help

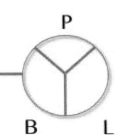

NEXT STEPS
- Summarize Offer Of Help
- Cost & Logistics
- Next Meeting Request

NOTES

DIRECTION

PREGAME
- Update Client Project Tracker
- Internalize Their Story
- Assemble Relevant Catalyst For Thought

WELCOME
- Agenda & Timeline

COMMON GROUND
- Balance Sheet
- Their Story Now

HEALTHY TENSION
- (In Light Of) Their Story Relative To The 3 Reference Points
- How Can The Type of Planning We Do Help
- Ideas/Options To Close The Gaps

NEXT STEPS
- Summarize Agreed Upon Path
- Cost, Logistics & Timeline
- Next Meeting

P

B   L

NOTES

EXECUTION

NOTES

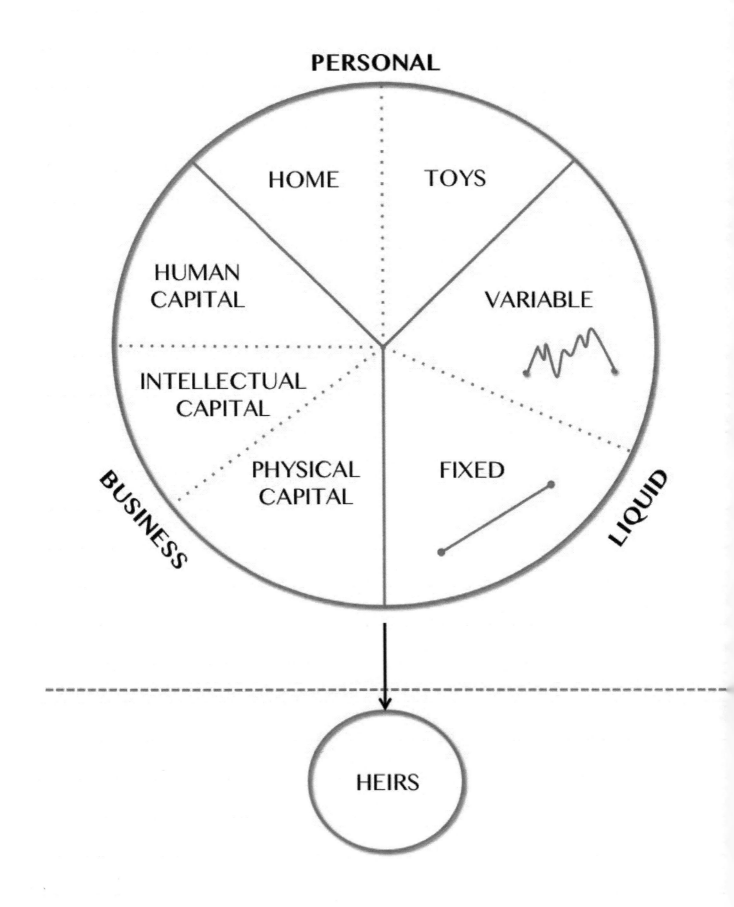

PERSONAL

HOME TOYS

HUMAN
CAPITAL

VARIABLE

INTELLECTUAL
CAPITAL

PHYSICAL
CAPITAL

FIXED

BUSINESS

LIQUID

HEIRS

NOTES

Being Rich Is The Activity Of Creating More Than You Consume

- ## Where Are They At Relative To Rich?
  - Thriving
  - Stabilizing
  - Surviving
- ## How Are They Navigating The 3 Reference Points To Rich?
  - Healthy Income
  - Build Value Outside Yourself
  - Impact Heirs

NOTES:

_____

_____

_____

_____

_____

_____

_____

_____

_____

_____

NOTES

Wesley Young is the founder of the financial consulting firm Wes Young & Associates. Wes specializes in building profitable, sustainable business operations. In addition to working with his private clients, he serves on the board of advisors to some of the nation's largest privately held companies. He is an author and speaker, receiving invitations to teach at churches, financial firms, business groups and leadership conferences across the country. Many have invested in and benefited from his audio and visual teaching as well as his books. Wes and his wife, Jamie, live in Austin, Texas, with their children Gage and Abby.

To book Wes for your event or workshop, call 512-329-4286.

For more information, go to www.WesleyYoung.com

- DISCLOSURES -